WE WERE TALKING ABOUT THE SPACE
BETWEEN US ALL.
—GEORGE HARRISON

# IN BETWEEN

POETRY COMICS BY

## MITA MAHATO

PLEAIDES PRESS

ISBN: 978-0-8071-6778-6

Published by Pleiades Press

Department of English
University of Central Missouri
Warrensbsurg, Missouri 64093

Distributed by Louisiana State University Press

Design and layout by David Wojciechowski, www.davidwojo.com
Author's photo by Allyce Andrew

First Pleiades Printing, 2017

Financial Assistance for this project has been provided by the Missouri Arts Council,
a state agency, and the National Endowment for the Arts.

FOR MA, WITHOUT WHOM

# CONTENTS

# 1 UNIDENTIFIED FEELING OBJECT

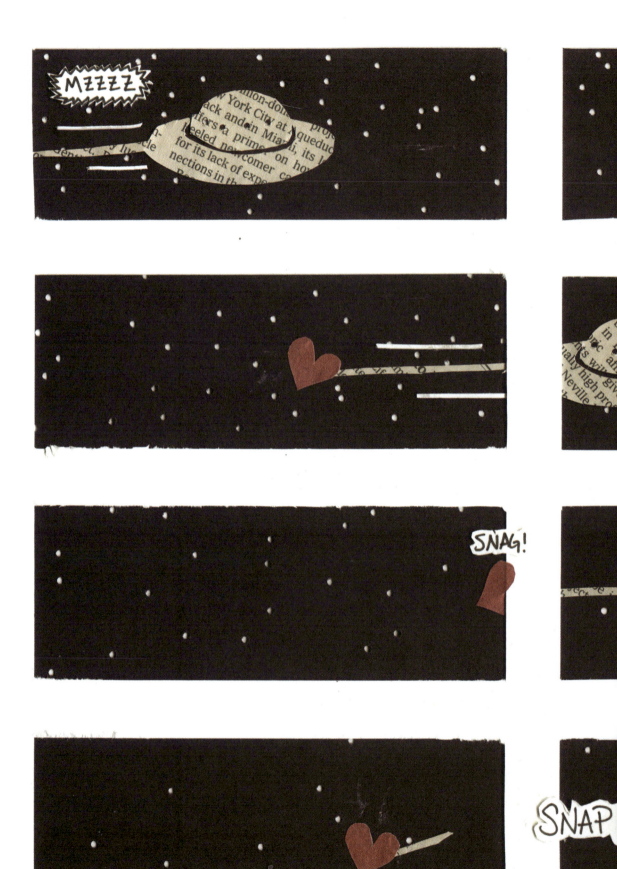

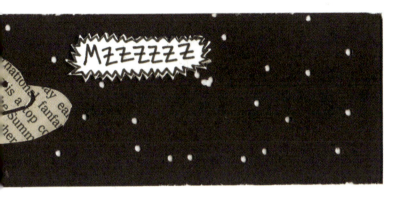

# 2 SEPTEMBER

Sometimes I wish
I could spend the month of
September
curled
up
in a
ball inside of a
HOLE

You see, every September for the last five years, I've had these terrible

nightmares about dying or death.

Once I had a dream about a dead man in a closet. A stranger. I may have been the one who killed him.

Last year, for the first time since the dreams began, you didn't appear as sick or dying or even like you ever had CANCER

But this time around the dreams all have this hospital blue tone to them so that even though you look young and vibrant, the dream itself looks sick.

That's when the dreams usually stop—after the anniversary of your death.

In the meantime, sleep is difficult, light is too bright, and life is buried deep beneath your absence.

# 3 THE SALMON

WE WATCHED A HUNDRED SALMON
DANCING — PINKS AND SILVERS —
FROM THE SIDE OF THE RIVER.

YOU MADE YOUR WAY UP A
SHALLOW FORK, STEADY FEET ON
SHAKY ROCKS, TO WHERE A FEW
LAY STRANDED.

THEIR TAILS FANNING POINTLESSLY — IT WAS PAINFUL TO WATCH.

YOU PICKED THEM UP ONE BY ONE AND HELPED THEM ON THEIR WAY.

will these branches

When will they

come back?

where did that bod

# 4 SOMETIMES YOU SEE ONLY WHAT YOU WANT TO SEE

# 5 PATTERNS

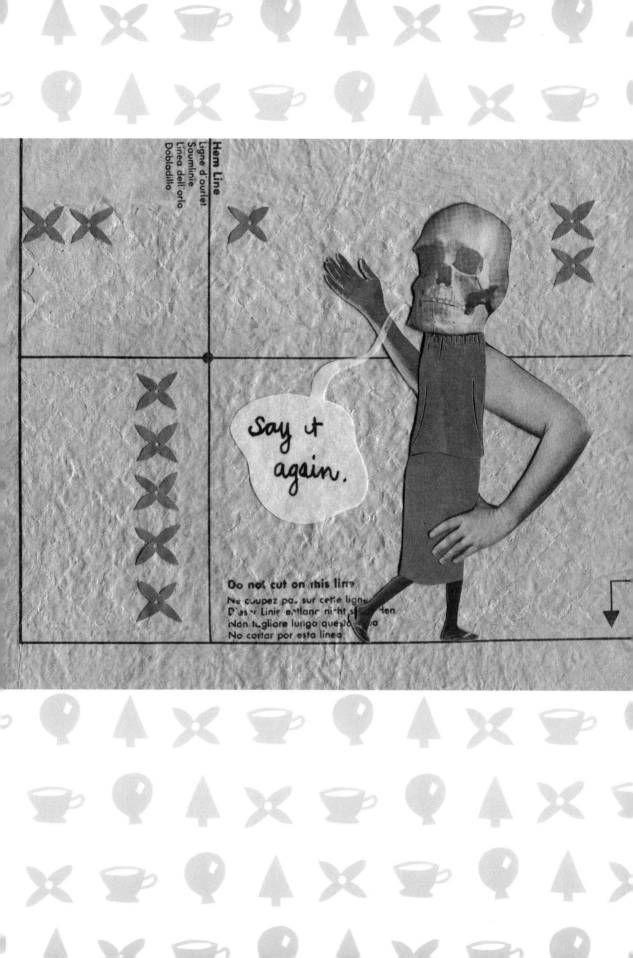

# 6 CAWS

# 7 BEACHED

# 8 THE EXTINCTION LIMERICKS

There once was a crow
from Hawaii.

There once was a tiger
from Java.

There once was a western black rhino.

There once was a dolphin named baiji.

# 9 BY THE DAWN

DREAD SILENCE REPOSES
HALF CONCEALS HALF DISCLOSES:

THE
GLOOM
OF THE
GRAVE,

OH SAY
CAN YOU
SEE?

OH SAY
YOU CAN
SEE.

## ACKNOWLEDGMENTS

This collection of comics represents the creative work of several years, as well as a different kind of work that happens within the shorter span of several months—selecting which comics to include, editing pieces to suit new page dimensions, and tackling the other odds and ends that go into book-making. For help received with these latter tasks, I owe many thanks: MK Czerwiec and Sarah Leavitt—thank you for holding me to deadlines and so much more. My continuing gratitude goes to Kelly Froh and Eroyn Franklin with Short Run Seattle, Michelle Hagewood at the Henry Art Gallery, Juliet McMullin and the Artist in Residence Program at the School of Medicine at UCR, and the University of Puget Sound. Along with those already mentioned, Mandolin Brassaw, Robyn Jordan, Emilie Bess, E.T. Russian, Janice Headley, Cindy Homan, Paula Knight, Jessica Hoffman, and Priti Joshi provided needed dialogue and advice, and I am grateful. Finally: Kathryn Nuernberger and David Wojciechowski—thank you for seeing poetry in my comics, and for your vision and trust.

MITA MAHATO is a Seattle-based cut paper, collage, and comics artist. Her cut paper work has been exhibited in galleries across the country and her comics and collaborative projects have been spotlighted by *The Stranger*, *Seattle Review of Books*, and *AV Club*. She is an Associate Professor of English at the University of Puget Sound, serves on the board for the arts organization Short Run Seattle, and is a teaching artist with the Henry Art Gallery.

www.TheseFramesAreHidingPlaces.com